Vivisection

& Other Poems

A collection by

Clinton W. Waters

ISBN-13: 978-1796289701

A Note from the Poet:

In your hands is a decade of my poetry, roughly from the end of high school through my late 20's, condensed down to 50 pieces. Many of them are appearing as I wrote them, with minimal modern revision.

I have always been someone who feels everything with a great intensity. You will see my younger self trying to get some of those feelings down on paper.

You'll take a trip to Germany where I studied abroad and felt so lonely I thought I might disappear.

You'll walk alongside the me that lost his brother and dad a year apart from one another.

You'll experience my first forays into love and exploring my queerness.

And you'll get a few that didn't really fit anywhere else.

I'm no longer the same me who wrote all of these poems, but as the person they grew into, I hope you enjoy their words.

I only ask that you be kind to these past me's (as I hope you are kind to your own past selves).

They are tender and kind, if not a bit foolish.

Thank you for reading. It means the world to me.

Love,

Clinton W. Waters

CONTENTS

I. Germany & Back Again

II. Grief, Death & Dying

III. Love & Longing

IV. Odds & Ends

I. Germany & Back Home Again

Angry Grapes

An insatiable wanderlust.
Blood rusting in veins.
Traffic lanes to be crossed,
feelings to be feigned

in some far off forest.
The nation whispers, “Go West.”
Its mouth on my earlobe, “California or bust,
‘though Oregon’s the best.”

I’ve got to feel lost again,
to sin or get sick, to feel
unfamiliar eyes pin “stranger”
to my chest as drawled vowels

drip from my lips. I need to rinse
this red, dead clay from my feet,
to dump dull dust from my hair,
to cleanse myself of Kentucky.

21 years of black-pepper gravy
and men asking how my mother’s been.
At my back, cows covered in feces
stare out from the black fences,

fences my brother and I painted
for our once step father, who sat
far out drinking tea in his truck
that was too wide for the road.

Okies and Arkies, wearing clothes
that are mostly pit-stains and sand,
cuss over busted, blown gaskets
but I cannot lend a mending hand.

I’ll reach the ocean by sunrise,
the moon waning at my approach.
I’ll read each star before it dies.

Essive

How much for a night?
How much to sleep
in a stranger's sheets
and wake up wondering

where you are? What
city have you wandered
to, and what is keeping
you there? Unbound

by roots like accents
or nostalgia, every room
is your room for however
many hours are paid. How

quickly people forget names
but how long the skin recalls
that moment when it was touched
and rippled out in bumps

in the night. How many blinds
until you find the ones that
shut out the flickering fluorescents
of the gas stations next door?

At what age does exploring become
escaping? Do you care to find out?

Glockenspiel Geister

Clockwork dancers spin
above, sashes frozen
in time by their crafter's hands,
fluttering in an imagined wind

that was squeezed between
grassy knolls and filtered
through black trees
that house amber eyes,

which hover above
fang-veiled mouths, dripping
with a craving for little
girls in red but might

settle for some boy from Kentucky.

The Altstadt, You Whore

Thousands of Roman soldiers
built what became
the Altstadt, the fortress
trading hands with whatever

leader or land wanted it
the most, or whoever
happened to remember
it was there.Like the oldest

girl in the harem that
was once the favorite.
Merchants threw up
houses with bloody money,

which have remained mostly
untouched for centuries.
But this fact doesn't
give you goosebumps

after the first time
you see a hobo throw
up in Arnuflsplatz
or see a handsome

man wearing a fashion
scarf (like every other
handsome man) sidle
up next to a buxomly babe

at the Film Buhne and
order her some liquory
concoction. The only

safe haven from
the verminous, teeming
hordes of pigeons is
St. Peter's Dom,

only because falcons
roost in the twin steeples
that took hundreds
of years to build.

Donau

The Danube slithers
downstream, carrying
ducks and debris to…
I don’t know where

(another on the laundry list
of things I should but do not know).

An impressionistic watercolor
of the inoffensively colored
buildings across the bank,
its mirror surface ripples

with movements of
something sinister and
cold, reptilian at best,
too bored to show its face.

When I stand at the edge,
it refuses to show my reflection.

The Devil in the Frauenkirche

"Right there," her voice
a respectful whisper
as the priest behind us
recites the scripture,

the words coated
in light that pours
into the hollow hall
from his left and right.

The Devil stomped
a crater in the entranceway
when he learned he
had been tricked,

that although he
held up his end of
the bargain (for once
the honest man),

the architect placed
a dozen windows
along the wall.But
from where he stood

and I stand now,
the windows are
invisible, a trick
of the eye.

I stop to wonder
why the Devil helped
build a church in the
first place. But it is clear

that I, like the Devil,
am easily fooled by perspective.

"Komm Schon"

The sun slinks toward
the horizon like a
one-night stand
hoping not to wake her,

although she's only
pretending to be asleep
because she can't remember
their name or recall

what country they come
from. Providing a rare
afternoon of unabated
heat, the sky having

forgotten it could clear,
the sun lingers a
moment, its reflection
stretched out like a lighter

flame or someone's shadow
as they stand in the doorway,
not sure if this farewell
is sufficient. But it sinks

away all the same, the townspeople
teeming in the new shadows,
surprised by the sudden chill,
only remembering its hot-breathed

request at the nape of their necks:
"Komm schon."
"Komm schon."

Summer Rain

Night gives no reprieve
to the heat, a thief of
breath and gumption
to those trapped between

the sagging buildings,
bulging at the bottom
like century-old glass,
solids settling like liquid.

Clouds canopy the city,
brooding, building up
but resisting the urge to
dump their deluge.

They tug at their collars,
soggy dollars pasted to
the inside of their pockets,
sweat clinging to the

backside of their knees.
There's tantric barometric
pressure, a dampness one
feels in-between their fingers

and the crooks of elbows,
the sensation of walking
through a steam cloud,
shortened breaths accidentally

catching whiffs of strangers
on the bus. A frenzy, furious
bees in their skulls, every pore
expanding in the haze until

finally the sky gives in to
its pent-up pleasure, sighing
in its pleasant defeat.

Upon Seeing the Pied Piper Moonlighting

The stomach of the
violinist outside the
shop loudly lurches,
unsatisfied with lunch.

His fingers don't know
a happy tune as tourists'
flip-flopped feet take
wide arcs to avoid his

open case, like his open
chest, barely covered
with clothes that he
doesn't remember buying.

He hopes to summon
a few Euros, but the
only thing he can think
to play is a somber song,

the whine of which
can conjure images
of long-limbed vampires
and blood-stained sleep walkers,

lingering in ancient archways
dancing between the haphazard
buildings that threaten to
lean in and kiss, although

it is not their cue. The sounds
swell and seep through the
arterial streets, bathing those
that may heed its moans.

But our violinist goes home
empty in more places than one,
his instrument a failing heart
his heart a failing instrument.

Passing Through

I can't stand them,
these transient places.
Airports, subway stations,
hotels, motels, malls.

Words slide down the walls
like graphic graffiti, lives
are lost like loose change
and shards of hearts litter

the floors, sentiments stain
the sheets that so many have
slept in already. Come morning
a uniform will wipe them clean,

will erase every bit of the people
that passed through.

ANOTHER STATE

"Oh Kentucky, why did you forsake me?"
-Regina Spektor

Oh Kentucky, why did I
forsake you? Forgive me
for I know not what I've
done. I miss your sensuous

slopes, the rise and fall
of your breast as you
escalate into summer,
your moist breath making

it hard to breathe. Let me
taste of the fencerow honeysuckle
and leave me alone to fend
off the crying cicadas.

I miss your many caverns,
threatening to collapse and take
us all with you into the dank
darkness, returning us to

the red clay from whence
we came. Allow me back
into the fold so that I
may speak your vowel-ridden

tongue and feel welcome
by complete strangers.
I'm sorry I said I'd rather
live in Arkansas, but you

know I didn't mean it.
Feed me country ham
and biscuits with gravy
so that I may grow fatter

for the impending winter,
your icicle trees and
sleet-slick streets seeping
their cold to the core of me.

I'll never leave again.

II. Grief, Death & Dying

"Are You Afraid of the Ones You Love?"

asked the radio into the hollow
husk of my car as it sped between
the lines. Amongst the sallow
static it asked once more,

somber and surreal.

Night wrapped around the
windows, my answer could
be yes…yes and only yes.
I'm terrified, dear radio,

dear Apophenia machine.
When the time is right,
a sickly and lean liturgy
of images come to mind,

a photobooth strip of mouths
agape, of arms crossed, hands
resting on chests, encased
in a pine box. Jewelry removed

and placed in pallid palms
before they are sunk into the
sea of earth carved out
just for them. Yes, sweet

radio, I cannot breathe
for the fear. Mortified
by their mortality; their
transience trickling terror,

cold-water streaks down
my spine. If you must
know, radio, my heart
is no stranger to skipping beats

or the rush of red thunder in my ears.

Gravamen

"Life s not fair,"
is written on a tombstone
somewhere in a neglected
churchyard, nestled amongst

the weeds. Polyester
flowers, faded and fake
as they may be, still
refuse to wilt or wither

atop the black stone.
Someone cared once,
to bear the flowers there,
but it has been some time

since living soles tread
the earth above him. It
is too painful to be reminded
of simple, staining thruths.

Take the time to know that
it rains on important days,
and your flat tire is not special.
Because in the mire of life

nothing is as awful as
a typo on a tombstone.

Inheritance

There are bodies
in our backyards,
brittle bones of strangers
sleeping beneath the soil.

Their heirlooms rot in
hidden homes amongst the ants.
Flowers grow red from the iron
in the plentiful, ancient veins

so rusted and full of rancor.

They’re waiting for you patiently,
all dolled up despite their dolor.

Potential

But what of time?
The less than a breath
it takes for potential to
become kinetic.

The difference between
an arrow in my hand,
an arrow on a bowstring,
and an arrow jutting from a deer.

Imagine a coin on a
thumb, either face
heavy with the weight
of decision and consequence.

Perhaps the most shocking
realization is that something
as immense as death

can come in something
as small as a bullet,
or a cyanide tablet,
or a dust mote.

These innocuous and
terribly terminal objects
laze about us,
humming and content

with their unused potential.

BLEED, BREATHE, EAT

(After Plath)

Ack! Mein Bruder,
I thought you were dead.

But there you stand
against the wall,

so tall and Aryan,
your eyes an infant blue.

There you are,
as you once were.

Eyes that once shone
now stab as I sway past
your gilded frame.

You have swathed
our mother's eyes

in soupy black tulle.
My how I –
how I hate you.

I'd kill you if the alcohol
hadn't done it first.

Instead, I drink your demise to give
honor to your amber assassin.

Meanwhile, you are their
Moloch, hungry and absent.

I –
I think I'll destroy your altar.

You'd still garner more praise than I
from beyond your writhing grave,

although I,
I, I, I
am the one
who bleeds, breathes, and eats.

Springtime in the Fatherland

People are dodging
dandelion dander,
picking it from their
teeth at the table

the way we'd sit
on the porch after
dinner, sucking at
our teeth and looking

at the stars. I would
probe at the veins
that ran atop his
arthritic wrists as

he told me stories
that only a few
Budweiser could
bring back from

their cloistered cell.
He told me why reading
aloud was bad luck and
why my friend had the

eyes of a witch, the
dirt floor drawl coming
out the longer we sat
and used up the sunlight.

Our words drifted up
like the airborne seeds,
helpless but not alone.

Yellow-Bodied Blue Rabbit

I am a gaudy glass
half-empty with
my father's blood.

I gained neither
his height nor
his cleaver nose;

my face is not his,
but neither is it my mother's.
I hardly believe it's mine.

I was gifted instead
with his penchant
for red-labeled booze.

I wasted my fourteen years
of biweekly visits on
Eastwood and Wayne

while he gazed at his mottled yard,
moldering in his melancholy,
smelling of oil and bakery bread.

I should have been
hoarding memories for
that fated Father's Day

when his blood ran cold,
the sluggish, icy red
settling in my veins.

HIS BED, THE KITCHEN TABLE

A cigarette smolders between
his fingers, smoke and smog
writhing up to brush the wrinkles
above his bushy brows. A grumble

mumbles from his mustached
lips, that inhale embers and
exhale sleep. Arrowhead chin
resting against his concave chest,

I wonder what he's dreaming.
The flame crawls down the
tube of tobacco, greedily gorging
on air, glowing in the guttural

gusting snores. Funeral pyre
ashes fall away from the gray
gyre and onto his uninspired
uniform. The one he hasn't bothered

taking off, for he will be in it
again in just a few fallow hours.
I watch the impending singe
as it nears the filter, sinking

into the cotton, so near to
those beer-soaked fingers.
Its molten kiss upon his
knuckles, he starts and

tries to suck the heat away
like poison. There is only
silence between us as
he smiles and lights another.

“Denn die Todten Reiten Schnell”

-from “Dracula” by Bram Stoker

The dead do not wear
the clothes that you give them.

No laughs ring from the graves
when your life is going well.

Formaldehyde brows do not furrow
in concern for your mortgage,

nor do hollow sockets
shed salty tears.

Their only shame is the
one that you give them.

For no thoughts swim
beneath the ground...

unless they belong to the
worms and the beetles, that is,

who burrow so busily
through wood and linen.

Just as we mine our memories
for scraps and souvenirs;

priceless because they're worthless.

III. Love & Longing

Love Songs of the Jackalope

The wandering fire moves
about, a pillar of flame in
the night to guide the lonely
ones through the cacti, bathed

in the shifting red that throws
their shadows about on the sand.
The hawks hunt by the light,
toads and mice swept away

in a flurry of feathers as
feet shuffle on. The jackalopes
watch wide-eyed, singing songs
they don’t know the words to.

I am amongst them, the exodus
seeking the flame that stays just
out of reach and I can’t help but
wonder: does it know where it’s going?

Immurement

Somewhere down the road
is a year of my childhood,
wandering out there in the woods
like the cat we left behind.

Between the tenuous trees
he wakes and weaves, wandering
where we have gone. And
through the eaves he sees

the house. Full of strangers,
full of things that are not his.
Who sleeps where he slept
beside the boy next door,

waking and wanting? Do
the whispers still hang in
the air? Do they cloud
dreams like they once did?

Since then he's found Jesus,
that boy next door. But that
shade amongst the trunks
and branches waits for him,

waits for another adventure
to see how deep they can go,
to find what treasures the trees
offer up to them amongst

the tangled roots. I need to find
him, to tell him the truth, to
release him from his toil. But
I've forgotten the way.

NERVES AND SKIN

Slide into the sheets,
shivering from the cold
and the unbearable
anticipation.

I think he heard it,
my every nerve and
scrap of skin
wanting his.

"It's so cold,"
he muttered
to the darkness.
So I drew him close.

Tongues roving
behind buck teeth,
we clutched, pressed
and shed.

"Are you sure that this
is what you want?"
his voice so close,
but his body closer.

The sensations
being far too much
for my body
to comprehend,

every nerve and
scrap of skin
cried out in
mirthful squeals.

Candlelit shower, we
foraged for some clothes
to sleep in,
his lips to my ear.

Problematica

Flip through the photos,
remember what you can,
super 8 films with hazy
edges that fill your mind.

And somewhere along
the way, things don't add
up. The dialogue you have
tucked away, collecting dust

in the folds, those words were
never spoken. There's bold print
on the broken cassette you keep
trying to play. The details you've

collected are wrong and he has
a separate set that are also just
as wrong. Your song never played
that night and the water in the pool

wasn't as cold as you think. His mom
was still awake, and yes she knows you
stole from her liquor cabinet. The feelings
weren't fake but the years have added

some sentimentality. The facts don't
match so you stuff them in the back.
Someday you'll see how they fit.
Someday you won't care.

Counting Ribs

Through the cloth, clutching hands,
the arching eyebrows and whisper-coated
palms can't pierce my whiskey aura, that
wafts off of me in waves. Yet you held

that hand. That hand that would later
trace endless circles between the hair,
under the cloth, while you lay
prostrate, the lump in your throat

the only thing moving. I counted
your ribs. The ribs that were covered
with nothing but sallow skin that
my ruddy fingerprints couldn't

stop tasting. I followed them
down the slope of your stomach,
a shallow pool. That shallow pool
whose surface my knuckles couldn't

disturb no matter how long
they lingered. Insatiate, I drew
you in and kept you, kept that
moment in a fold. A fold

that refuses to reconcile.

Pyrophoric

Haunted by the living,
each flaunted newborn
and engagement ring is a
match that's burning down

to my gnawn off nails. I light
penny votives, praying not
to feel your skinny phantom
limbs tangling with mine.

But there you are, sweet stench
of up-all-night breath in the
fickle flicker of the fire, your
cheekbones digging into my

chest. I can get no rest until
I've done my penance, recounted
the missed kiss in the driveway,
winced at how everything I wanted

was you. In the dying light, I let
the memories' heat eat me from
head to feet. My flabby frame
goes up like tender tinder, flames

fueled by thoughts like how much
I loved you on the back porch that
night and how I needed you so bad
it wrung my insides out. A witch

upon a stake, I could douse the
blaze and save myself, just let you
drift away. But I know the burn will
fade, pain will turn to detached

observance. In the morning I'll
poke through the ashes, wash away
the bonfire smoke and salvage
enough to get up, knowing you'll be

close, gas can in hand.

My Baby was Hungry, but

there were loan sharks swimming
in the crabgrass lawn,

where weeds poked through
bicycle spokes and headlines
faded on waterlogged newsprint.

My baby was hungry, and
the phone wouldn't stop its
ringing, 'cause miles away

some lady was waiting for the
answering machine like she was
waiting on her nails to dry,

so she could read from
the script and make empty
threats about foreclosure.

My baby was hungry, but
he was warned not to use
the stove 'til they got back.

Sometimes he'd wake up
and find them in their bed
or watching the morning news,

coming and going like cicadas.

He grew up hungry
for voices that didn't
come out of the T.V.,
doors that didn't stay locked;
anything that was more than half-hearted.

My baby's got a pocket-full
of food he'll never eat.

My baby is insatiable.

Saint Hubertus

He looks down on them
from his arbor perch,
doused in misleading scents
and swathed in sneaky leaves.

This boy whose hair has
lost its golden tint without
the sun's persistent nagging,
only to be dyed red for pageantry

and looks a bit like red velvet cake
as he puts arrow to bow,
fingers to string and
fist to beating breast.

A stag saunters below,
surrounded by his harem
of daintily dotted does.

In an instant the stag's features
shift to that of a boy,
someone Red Velvet knows
from afar and from within.

Deerboy smiles, an ambient
glow swathing his nude frame.
He raises both hands,
enticing and inviting.

The arrow flies, uninterested
in Red Velvet's reticence.

KOLIBRI

You bore.
You tease.
You down-right brute.

We are faithfully facing forward,
our elbows touching,
without expression-as if
nothing's happening…

because "nothing is happening."

You flash those fangs
and guffaw at my words
that you don't really know
or care to know.

You talk and talk
and blur the lines
that have been drawn.
You know exactly what you do.

But I tell you this,
when you tire of what we've
been up to all along,
you'll prod and purge

with your long knives.

But

I will not get up.
I will not get dressed.
I will not stray from these sheets.

PREDATOR/PREY

Barn-cat eyes swivel
in your skull and settle
on my swollen fingers,
bloodied by tactless teeth.

You flash fox fangs
at a twittering tongue
as it totters about
in my meager mouse mouth.

Peeling off layers of pretense,
you shamelessly splinter
my shedding snake skin,
revealing the soft underneath.

Hearts beat at a jackrabbit pace,
awaiting a bear-trap embrace.

Downtown Morality

Feeling my soul recede from
my fingertips. Watching you
through these bleary orbs,
I fear I'm losing control.

The band's swaying, singer
lit from below so his glasses
make black thorn horn shadows
across his sweaty head. I can't

see the crowd for the jerking
bodies. I'm spiraling behind
my eyes and if I'm going to crash
I'm taking someone with me.

Strolling through the no-man's-land,
I slip a hand onto your back, offer
a drink I can't afford. Good lord
we're standing in a puddle of God

knows what, but who cares? This
downtown morality's in effect and
there's finality in the wrecked attempts
to make last call. They're leaving in

pairs and it's our turn. I'll lick the
smoke from your lips if you'll let me.
We can stumble down the street
to wherever, your place or mine.

The promised land is turning off the
neon and the founts are running dry.
Let's lie together and lie about our
names. Let's whisper prayers in the dark.

Ensnared

There’s kindling in
the back of my throat
as I lap up last night’s
cologne from the base

of your outstretched neck.
So smooth, so couth
as it rumbles with
gasps and giddy groans.

Come, I’ll help you
map out your moles
as you calmly count
my fingers and toes.

All the while we’ll say,
“I do not pine,
I do not pray for you,”

as we enjoy the trainwreck
of our tangled limbs.

A Cathedral of Nature

The sounds of the city
cannot pierce the
cathedral's columns,
their bases buckling

from the effort.
The eaves of leaves
shudder above, their
limbs crawling with

living creatures that I
cannot see from the
ground, but watch over
me all the same.

The air glows green
with slanted light
striking the stained-glass
panes of chlorophyll

as I walk along the
hedgerow pews, having
impure thoughts of you
at the sight of

lazy heads lolling in
their lover's lap, hair
brushed back and lips traced
with careful, calloused fingers.

Imagine us kneeling
behind trees, praying to
the holiness inherent
in muscles and mouths.

The trunks tremor with
tumors, as if the city
has finally gotten under
their scaly skin.

I know how they feel.

ANADIPSIA

It is likely that the
water you seek
will do little to
sate your thirst.

Heaving breaths
in a back room
can very easily
become sighs.

A new job will
still not pay you
the few thousand
you think you need

and you are wont
to love others more
than they could
ever deserve or return.

For we walk the
same desert, tricked
by the same shimmering
mirages. Crawling from

one oasis to the next.

Tinder Skeleton

The flame in the fireplace
shifts its tinder skeleton,
its blue belly shifting as
it settles in to tell the tale

of its fathers and forefathers.
Sparks flying from flint
becoming the consuming
cherry of a cigarette, a finite

life clutching the cotton
as it smoldered into obscurity.
Yet others, in their gluttonous
lust for life, devoured whole

forests, tree lines alive with
their form as their progeny
crept down hills and into homes.
If only he could do something

great, he crackles and sighs
to the candles on their sticks.
But they hold no mercy,
once burned by old flames

that took them for their
worth, twice shy to try
again. The misery
pooled around their feet,

their bent wicks curled,
they know they'll do it again.

Animism

We bared our teeth
and beat our breasts
until they flushed bright red.

We compared physiques
as if to determine the worth
of the oncoming events.

We closed the distance
and clashed in a burst
of good intentions,

wailing and biting
at every inch of flesh
intimate and immediate.

This carried on until
our skin was painted
with cherry blossom bruises.

We panted and snarled,
licking wounds and feeling
utterly disappointed.

Cannibals!

It would seem that
Cannibalism is all the rage
amongst the men and women
of this place called here.

They stuff one another
into their moist maws
and swallow them whole,
just to expect the same;

to devour and be devoured,
as if it's fun and games.

However, I, like the
Uroboros, am left to
eat none other than myself
in a fickle, cyclical manner.

Oh, how I grow weary of
the taste of my choosy chastity,
drizzled with self-worth
on a leafy bed of esteem.

The candelabra burns
with an admirable ardor
as I dine with Disdain,
awaiting our third ~~course~~ guest

whoever that may be.

Skinner Box

The ocean is coming to get us.
We watch the waves, furling
and curling like the folds
of a lover’s clothes

as its yawn becomes our yawns.
Stretched limbs and guttural groans
prompt a response but I
don’t know the right one.

I’m having trouble finding
the button, the way to a reward.
Shouldn’t it be red?
Shouldn’t there be some sort of label?

Knees bump clumsily and
linger as fingers prod soft spots,
all to no avail.

I’ve got to find it.

The ocean is coming to get us
and you haven’t moved an inch.

The Sea is Singing Yellow Songs in Time

to bellows breathing below sickly ships.
It rises, phantom floating man-o-wars,
askew in tides, in waves it makes, induced
with giddy, hopeful, muffled voices lost

in sheets and showers, hotel rooms and pools.
It surges, liquor bubbles popping twice
to fashion measures, beats and tone. Inside
small cabinets and armoires, silver tunes

brush lonely lingerie and sexy things
that did not make the cut. A song for those
that feel and know its lyrics already,
it dances through the veins from mouth to groin

to mouth again, excels at moving feet
and hands in executing what they want.
Dumb ears on either side of my head hear
the tune but rhythm loses footing here.

Yet still the hum that swims about my sleep
can feel its humming heartbeat in my hands
and flounders near the life and faithful lines
that flow across the palms and disappear.

You and I

Blue-tinted kisses at dawn,
before the sun sets trees ablaze.
Oh how I've missed this. This
bleary bliss. Fighting to keep

the cold outside the blankets.
Wide grins and "Do that again."s.
The snap of your glasses lens,
Oh how sorry I've been.

Oh how many wishes does it take
to make this last? To keep these
minutes from the past. To keep
touching for touching's sake.

To see you above, below, beside me.
Oh how am I supposed to leave?
Your rumbling whispers, my bumbling
fingers. Tumble with me through space.

VIVISECTION

If you were to
split me apart,
cleave me in two
with your hatchet tongue,

what might spill out?

They split the atom
and look at what happened.
Could the things within
turn you to ash?

Could the heartsick
flame inside my stomach
eat you up? Could it pin your
silhouette to the floor?

Perhaps all the words
I've swallowed for you
would make their bloody revolt
and swarm about like flies:

A haze of Scrabble pieces
vying for entry to your soul,

to fill your belly
like they've filled mine
making it bulge and stretch
into something cumbersome.

The films behind my eyes
would tumble out,
a Gatling gun slideshow
of memories and dreams:

a dog's bloody mouth
beer on your breath
a candle in a Hostess cake
your head on my shoulder
a smoldering cigarette in a sleeping hand
and on and on and on

Until you're tarred with
my neuroses and
feathered with all
these phobias.

Finally I will be
hollow
and horribly content.

IV. Odds & Ends

“AMERICA BLEEDS GOD”

states the bold block
letters on a bumper
glued to the back
of some jalopy, which is
double-parked on the curb

outside a tittie bar,
where lonely men sit on stools
and spend money they don’t have
to get simulated affection
from women who pay

bills with sweaty bills
that swap from hand
to hand, heavy with
their abstract values
established by a

swarm of suits
in a place you’ve never seen
that is managed by people
whose names you do not know
but pass rules and regulations

on ideas more abstract than
the $4.95 it took to buy
a senseless sticker proclaiming
that a nation cannot only bleed,
but when it does, a deity

flows forth.

Broadway Ave, 2 AM

There's a wrinkle
in the neon and
eyes between
the blinds upstairs.

In these hours
that can be seen
as early or late
(depending on the job)

headlights become
basilisk glares that freeze
pell-mell pedestrians in
their lopsided footprints.

They stumble home,
afraid you're some cop
come to make them touch
the tip of their noses,

noses that are inhaling
an undertaker's
hard work in the kilns,
transferring flesh to ash.

He's letting someone's soul
seep and slip out of the chimney
in serpentine corkscrews.

CONSTRUCTING A LOLLIPOP MAN

Want to make yourself a man
without corpses, criminal brains
or possible peasant riots?

It's easy!

You will need:

1. Sugar for his words,
2. Corn Syrup dripping from his teeth.
3. Partially Hydrogenated Soybean Oil (Whatever the hell that is).
4. Citric Acid in his belly.
5. Condensed Soy Milk remembered by his tongue.
6. Cocoa for his skin, which tastes of Artificial and Natural Flavors. (It's hard to find Artificial Colors. They all look so real.)

Put into a bowl and blend until smooth.

Somehow these things come together.
Through some culinary, alchemic black magic,
a whole is made from the sum of parts,
the way two frisky gametes fused to make you.

Pour into a mold and wait for a thunderstorm.

Tell assistant to flip various switches
and raise the platform.

When lightning strikes your creation,
lower said platform.

Let stand for at least ten minutes.

Shout in triumph.
Something like "IT'S ALIVE" will do.

Exoskeleton

Warm weather has come
and it has summoned
an horrific hum
that rises from the chlorophyll.

Thoraxes squirm and antennae
writhe upon your appearance.
They can taste you.
They can breathe you in like air.

Stepping into this drone
of incessant wings
and clenching pincers,
you become their roasted swine:

succulent and scintillating.

The ants erupt from their
catacombs, a trail of endless
ellipses that are hungry
for your saccharine sugar.

The ticks are navigating
hairs on your leg,
a pilgrimage to your groin,
thirsty for your blood.

The bees, fat and fearless,
pulse with the insatiable
urge to pierce your skin
and die some sort of useful death.

Even the butterflies,
spreading their wings wide,
are staring down at you
twitching their impatient snouts.

They all envy your flesh,
jealous of your hidden bones.
They are ashamed of
their blatant outer shells.

Fonts

And it dripped
from your lips
like desirous drool,

the shamefully steady flow
Of who, what, and where
that covered our floral wallpaper

in an excess of excuses.

Adjectives, adverbs and antecedents
spewed out in Calibri and Cambria,
and seeped into the threadbare sheets.

Ugh, those stains will never come out.

Your typewriter tongue clacked
a machine-gun rattle so that
the carpet matched the drapes:

the whole house done up
in shades of woe-is-me.

Midge Gillars in her Grave

I taught them my tongue,
those youths talented
in the world's gibberish;

the language that had
told me "no" just one
too many times.

They drank my words,
unknowing of their power
to bend, break, coddle or accuse.

So skilled was I in my
treacherous and heartbreaking
dialect, men swathed in

lightning bolts and black leather
offered me a throne upon
a radio tower, its waves
carrying my voice for miles.

Gravelly with cigarettes and seduction,
my mouth rested on the invaders'
shallow, shell-shocked ears.

Impersonating their mothers
I wailed over their imminent deaths,
and how their girls were on
their backs in some boy's car.

However, my threats weren't enough
to keep them from crossing borders.

Showered in red and black
banners I ran back to the grizzled
wolf's teat, that land I thought I had escaped.

The fools, they charged me with eight counts,
although there were certainly ten or more,
only one of which earned me a conviction
by a jury of my "peers",

as if they couldn't count.

Amongst careful habits and rosaries, I died.
A passing utterly unfit for the
Bitch of Berlin.

SHE'LL GET HERS.

She was born with her heart
on her sleeve. Bulls-eye red,
her mother said,
the better for others to take aim.

So she painted it blue.

That haint blue heart of hers
repelled the forces of
thought and memory;
two black birds circling,

watching and recording
for those too lazy to see
the world for themselves,
those lost in thunderclouds
and black lightning.

She and her haint blue heart,
they were going somewhere;
somewhere away from the exposed ribs
of funeral home awnings

and the smell of wasted time
lingering on the petals of daisies
in the hair of pretty girls who
clung to their men,

desperation dressed up as
playing princess and planning weddings.

When she returned, her haint blue heart
in its cardboard suitcase, she arrived
with delightfully dry eyes,
wide and worldly.

"My, what big eyes you have,"
the townsfolk remarked.

"The better to see your graves."

Ver'Lor

(After Lovecraft)

I seek him, the one exiled
to the horizon. Ver'lor,
Mountain of the Mind,
Shadow on the Sea,
who has come to me
in dreams, has whispered
in my ear from his
perch upon the line
where earth meets sky
and when I close my eyes
I can feel his wretched breath,
the death of hundreds wafting
up from his guts that yearn
for more. I seek him in his
palatial prison, the world
set aside from this one where
he bides the centuries that
go by, waiting to be forgotten,
waiting for his return.

SERVANT

Her tiny tyrant wails
from his crib, yearning
for milk, attention, maybe
a crisp new diaper.

Perhaps he is crying
just to make noise.

His face appears over the rail,
fervent and red. Crocodile tears
stream down in rolling rivulets,
converging in his dimpled chin;

the chin his father gave him,
wherever he may be...

He bends and flails, adding weight
to her weary and woeful arms,
which strain against their invisible
shackles labeled “duty” and “love”.

But once he starts to slumber
and that malicious mouth shuts
he resembles something beautiful-
although he certainly isn't.

She strokes his fevered forehead,
mustering some motherly feeling,
thinking to herself,

“You're hardly a servant
if you enjoy the work.”

ABOUT THE AUTHOR

Born and raised in Bowling Green, KY, Clinton W. Waters holds a degree in Creative Writing from W.K.U. Their work has been featured in university publications from W.K.U., University of Regensburg, and Still: The Journal.

OTHER WORKS BY CLINTON W. WATERS

-30-

It's Greg's birthday. His 30th birthday. The birthday that will determine the rest of his life. At midnight, there is the chance Greg will simply cease to exist. With that in mind, he has hired Joe, an Ephemera, to accompany him on what might be his last day on earth. What starts as a rented relationship soon becomes more complicated.

Is it possible to fall in love in less than 24 hours? Is there a point if one of them might not be alive at midnight? Greg can only be certain of one thing: the clock is ticking.

INVERT

In an alternative history 1950s, where atomic war was waged on the US during World War II, birth rates are dangerously low. As a result, The Department of Virtue was founded to ensure that not only are people procreating, but they're doing it the right way. The Virtuous Family is a ubiquitous reminder of all that Americans should strive to be.

Greer's life is ruled by the DOV. An invert reformed in one of the nation's many Sanctuaries, he is employed as a "Screw" (Sex Crime Worker). It's his job to entrap other men into making advances so they can be arrested and similarly "reformed". His wife, Alice, is a cured invert as well, prescribed by the state and ordered to attempt procreation. By chance, they have met another invert couple, Bill and Sally. Their romance must remain a secret, or else they may not be given another chance. For Greer, there are eyes in every window and shadows down every side street waiting to catch him slip.

When Greer is assigned Matthews as a new partner, he has to wonder if this man is a plant, meant to keep an eye on him, or if this new Screw is just another victim of Virtue.

(UN)Bury Your Gays

This collection compiles the novella (Un)Bury Your Gays and six other short stories. Reanimated best friends, monsters beneath the kitchen sink, desires made manifest, creek creatures, 80s cyberpunk, ghosts, and crashed alien ships all find homes between the pages of this anthology.

It's the late 2000's. Humphrey West and his best friend Danny are just trying to survive their senior year. Unfortunately, Danny falls short of that goal after a risky rendezvous. But Humphrey has just the thing: a concoction borne of magic and science that is able to bring the dead back to life (at least it's worked on a bee so far). Against all odds, Danny comes back from the clutches of death.

The Danny that returns is...different. And it's not just the missing memories. Soon, Humphrey is doing everything in his power to keep his friend alive, but none the wiser to what is happening.

A SAMPLE FROM
-30-

Morning

The door creaked open and so did Greg's eyelids. It was blue dawn and socked feet padded their way past his back to the foot of the bed. Greg's phone illuminated his cocoon of comforter, alerting him that his Ephemera, Joe, had arrived. Joe was putting his jacket on the back of the chair at Greg's desk. "Right on time," Greg groaned. They had agreed on the terms of their engagement a few days prior, and Joe was holding true to them. It had felt odd to Greg, giving a stranger the code to get into his apartment. But then again, this was all a little strange.

"You don't get five stars by being late," Joe whispered. Greg could hear the smile in his voice and it made his stomach sweetly sour. How long had it been since someone new was in his bedroom? Leftover dreams clung to the corners of his mind as he rubbed his eyes. When he opened them again, he saw that Joe's stomach was sky blue in the pale light of the morning, his shirt lifting up and over his head. He folded it and draped it over his jacket. His belt buckle clinked as he undid the clasp, jingling as he took off his pants and folded them neatly. He laid them over the back of the chair as well.

Checking the time, Greg did some foggy-brained math and determined he had only gotten a few hours of sleep. Unable to feel tired for the anxiety of it all, he had performed the cardinal sin of trying to do research online, as if that would put his mind at ease. He had done so well up until that point, only the occasional deep dive every few years. He read articles and seriously considered buying some ebooks on the matter. Bombarded by ads for life insurance with sad songs about heaven, he gave up. He wound up at the same conclusion everyone had told him for years. It would never make sense. There would be no correlation. No demographic data that skewed one way or the other. No probability model of lifestyle or location that could give him an honest answer. It all amounted to 50-50.

A coin that had been spinning mid-air for 30 years.

He chuckled to himself at that thought. He was showing his age. Coins. What a novel concept.
Greg sank a little towards the middle of the mattress as Joe sat on the side. “May I join you?” he asked. He turned to look at Greg over his shoulder, which was mottled with pale freckles, tiny hairs glowing as the blue gave way to red and orange. Greg was surprised at how broad Joe was, taller and larger than he had imagined from his pictures on the Ephemera app. He had little love handles that rested above the waistband of his boxers, dark pink stretch marks rising up from below. Greg lifted the comforter and Joe slid in so that they were face to face. The comforter descended again and plunged them into darkness. Just Greg’s morning breath mingling with the coffee clinging to Joe’s teeth..

“Happy Birthday,” Joe said quietly.

“What’s so happy about it?” Greg asked, his voice gravelly. He had paid for an entire day. The moment he woke up until just past midnight that night. Had paid extra to ensure midnight was included in their allotted time. From there, whether Greg disappeared or went on living didn't matter. They'd never see each other again. Maybe it never mattered, he thought to himself.

"It's yours, for one," Joe said. He placed a leg over Greg's and pulled up the hem of Greg's shirt, resting his hand on Greg's side. Greg jerked at the cold of it and they both laughed. He felt a bit of the awkwardness ebb away. But this stranger, this Joe was in a spot that had belonged to someone else.

"What about for two?" Greg asked.

"For two, you have me," Joe said into the darkness. Greg's phone illuminated again, a happy birthday text from Avni. Of course she'd be texting him this early. He felt a little silly, but the thought did occur to him that he was excited for her to meet Joe. Maybe that equated to showing Joe off, which didn't make him feel great. But then again, wasn't that a perk of having him in the first place?

Bathed in the dull white glow, Greg begrudgingly admitted to himself how handsome Joe was. How that had been a major factor in choosing which Ephemera he'd spend his 30th birthday with. But more than how attractive he was, Greg felt he "looked" like a boyfriend. The kind who had family out west and had bad taste in music, but called it artistic. Someone to crawl into bed in the wee hours of the morning and stick his cold mitts on your stomach. The kind of guy Greg would take to dinner at his mom's house (an event he would absolutely dread, but Joe would genuinely look forward to). For a moment, the cell phone's light reflected in Joe's dark eyes, and he thought of looking across the table at him and giving him a pained look as his mother veered into politics. He was taking a memory of Zeke and imposing Joe on top of it. It was working perhaps too well.

The light grew dim and shut off, waking Greg up from his daydream.

He thought of the reality. Saying goodbye to his mother the day before. Just in case. Asking her not to come to the party. The pain in her eyes, how her lips grew thin with the effort of biting her tongue. Him bringing up the only other party they had both been at, Alissa's, four years ago.

He took a deep breath and sighed at this.

"And for three, I have the whole day planned out," Joe said, "nothing for you to worry about." This was part of their ruse, however. A line he had given Joe to feed him. Greg had actually planned the entire day, more or less. But Joe was going to handle everything. Carry the bags. Help him decorate for the party. Greg began to think about the party then, his heart beating a little quicker. God, there was so much left to do. "Hey," Joe said, almost sternly. "Don't spend today worrying, okay?" he said, his hand roving under Greg's shirt. He drew Greg closer to him, his lips finding Greg's in the dark. He kissed him softly, their lips just barely brushing. Greg returned the gesture with force, bringing a hand up to rest on the back of Joe's head. Greg felt as though he should pull away. This was all a lie. A lie he had paid for. But he was ashamed at how quickly his body was ready to accept it, felt starved and wretched.

His face grew hot, embarrassed at how pitiful he was. Paying for someone else's company. Joe squeezed him and he said, "Okay?" in a deep grumble.

"Okay," Greg said, relenting and burying his face in Joe's neck. He had the sudden urge to cry. Why not, he figured. He may not have that many opportunities left.

"It will be a good day," Joe said. His arms softened from grip to comforting embrace. "I promise," he whispered. What a way to ruin the mood, Greg thought to himself as he blubbered. But maybe he was a little grateful, a little glad sex wasn't the first thing they did together.

The sun had officially climbed over the horizon by the time Greg's tears ran dry. Joe kissed him on the forehead and slid out of bed. Greg finally emerged from the comforter, eyes red and puffy. "I'm going to get started on breakfast," Joe said, reaching for his clothes.

"Don't," Greg said. Joe smiled and bowed his head slightly. He stood and left. A few moments later Greg heard the clattering of dishes. Greg pulled himself out of bed and stood at his window for a moment. The world outside was well awake by now. Fat flakes of snow were falling lazily from the sky and Greg felt a surge of happiness. He had really been hoping to see snow on his birthday.

A SAMPLE FROM INVERT

The Virtuous Family

Greer sat at a table, waiting for his mark. It was a spooky place and it made him uneasy. Red glass centerpieces with little votive candles threw weird shadows everywhere and cast everything in a bloody hue. Strands of tinsel were strung up, still and glittering in the stagnant, smoke-filled air. Greer had been in plenty of these little hole in the wall places over his four years in the service. But this one gave him the blues. Sad men in a sad place, trying to hide their sad little malediction.

He sat alone, as did all the other men in the bar. A tired lady in a red dress was more or less singing some tune while a skinny man in tight pants and a Santa hat played an equally tired looking piano. She knew she was set dressing. The one woman who kept this place from being an illegal gathering. This tracked. He had noticed they were a skittish bunch. The Surveillance creeps had him coming every couple of nights. What hypocrites, he thought to himself. Perverts watching other perverts. The difference was they had badges and these poor bastards didn't.
He had taken a couple guys for a walk through the nearby alleys. Luckily none of them were brave enough to make a move. He pitied them and their nervous jabber. Their hunger clearly etched in their mournful frowns. Their licked lips. Their tugged groins.

But never an overt physical come on. That's what would get them scooped. The crime was the "committing of an action concurrent with homosexual gratification". The U.S. government and their Department of Virtue hadn't outlawed wanting it. Not yet, anyway. If they had a way to read minds Greer was sure it would be up there with murder.

He was grateful they were triggershy. It wouldn't do for the others to put two and two together. Enough of them go missing or get arrested and they move. Like rats, he thought. Greer needed a specific rodent to take the bait in order to meet his quota. A Mr. Ira Sanderson. Politician type. Not the mayor but someone close. Greer didn't really read the papers. He took a sip of his whiskey, barely a drop passing his lips. He didn't like to be drunk on the job.

An older fella had been giving Greer the eye for the better part of a half hour. He kept licking his lips like he might eat Greer whole. Looking to the door, Greer was more than halfway relieved to see his target had finally decided to show up. The little bartender had just made last call. His mark was smart. Or at least cautious. He could snag one of these marys as they left. Happen to walk home in the same direction. Plausible deniability.

Greer snubbed most of a good cigarette out, which hurt him. He'd get more in his monthly allotment, but that felt like years away. And it would only come if he got this particular collar. He made eye contact with Sanderson, who had yet to take off his coat. Good, he was in a hurry too.

Kicking his chair back softly, Greer stood. He threw some change on the table. He kept his eyes trained on Sanderson's as he stepped towards the door. So far so good. The "singer" was packing it in and the pianist was lowering the key cover.

Sanderson took a step, trying to get out of Greer's way. Greer got close instead, reaching over Sanderson's shoulder to get his coat. He had to be careful. If he was the first to initiate touch, it would all be worthless. The red light and his thin mustache made Sanderson look like a devil from the cartoons. Come to tempt a man into a sinful act. Greer winked. Sanderson smiled.

Greer went through the door, into the cold night. He made it up the stairs to street level before he looked back. Sanderson stood in the doorway watching him. Greer tilted his head back. Sanderson started up the stairs.

Greer walked along the road for a minute. He stopped and Sanderson stopped too, about six feet back. Greer feigned having trouble keeping a match lit long enough to light his cigarette. Sanderson swooped in. He flicked a gold lighter into life and held it beneath the cigarette's tip. His teeth were orange in the fire's light. Greer thanked him. Sanderson started walking down a nearby alley. Damn. Greer wasn't leading the dance anymore. But no matter. Whatever this guy needed to feel comfortable enough to kiss or touch him. Greer followed Sanderson for a bit, careful to keep a map in his head of how to get back to the street in case things went sideways.

He turned a corner and found Sanderson in a dead end, surrounded by garbage cans and darkness. This was it. "What's your name?" Sanderson asked with a grin. Greer gave him something. "I like that," Sanderson said as he undid the button on his pants. "Come here," he said. Greer looked around, playing scared. He used that time to ensure an officer had followed them. Sure enough, he saw Jenkins creeping towards him. "No one will find out," Sanderson whispered. Greer smiled and moved close. Careful. Don't touch him. Sanderson pushed his pants down and Greer swallowed, trying not to look down. "It's all right," Sanderson said quietly. Sanderson grabbed Greer's hand and put it on his crotch. Greer felt the warmth and screwed his eyes shut tight. Bile-diffused whiskey came up in the back of his throat.

"Hands up!" Jenkins yelled from behind Greer. Greer complied immediately, backing away. Someone from Surveillance was there, snapping pictures. Sanderson floundered, trying to yank his pants up. Jenkins "arrested" Greer first. He pushed him into the nearby brick wall and mashed his face against it. His cheek burned as the brick bit into it. When he got apprehended along with his marks, he found every beatwalker did it differently. None of them were his friends, wouldn't be. But there were assholes like Jenkins who enjoyed making it more painful than it had to be. "It's gotta be believable," he said the last time Greer confronted him about it. He had also spat a wad of phlegm at his feet for extra measure.

"We'll be taking you both in for questioning," Jenkins said, wrapping the cuffs around Sanderson's wrists. He was spluttering. Saying how they didn't have to do this. He had been a friend to the police department for many years. "Save it for the judge,"

Jenkins said, yanking Sanderson forward, then peeling Greer off the wall.

They rode in the back of the police car in total silence. Greer hazarded a single glance at Sanderson, but the man was distraught. "I'm sorry," he finally said, tears streaming down his face. "I got you mixed up in all this." Greer was stunned. Over the years, his fake arrests did their job of putting up appearances, in case his collars went on to blab. But none of them had ever apologized to him. "My wife is going to kill me," Sanderson said to himself. Greer watched him press his forehead to the window and let out a whimper. It made Greer's lip curl in disgust. No, Greer thought. You won't die. You may wish you had at some point. But the Sanctuaries had a way of turning you around. Making sure your insides matched your outsides. You just had to survive until you got to that point. Sanderson being married already would help. Greer didn't know if he had a child, but if they had managed to conceive at some point, all the better. He'll be just fine, Greer thought to himself.

Once inside the precinct, they were led to separate rooms. Greer's handcuffs were removed and he jotted down some information in a log book. The officer on desk duty that night wouldn't look at him. "Have a good one," Greer said, feeling like being an asshole. The officer pretended not to hear, slamming the log book closed and taking it off to wherever it lived. He muttered, the only thing Greer catching for certain was "invert".

Greer stepped out onto the street. The cold

wind on his inflamed face felt good. He touched the wound and his fingers came away with just a little bit of blood. He'd had worse. He took his time getting to the DOV. Once inside, the night clerk looked over his badge before letting him through another set of interior doors. As if the man hadn't seen him come in countless times.

The place was clean in a gross way. Like a church or a hospital. How meticulously some people had to work to make this place look this good. He paused to look at the mural that took up the entire back wall. You could see it from the street, but no one would really need to. Their posters and ads in the newspapers used it, and images like it, over and over again. They prescribed what every citizen should strive for. Men worked, stoic guardians of their home and country. Women served and created happy homes. They both were expected to create more Americans, to ensure these virtues were passed on and propagated.

A man and woman stood, admiring the stars and stripes. The man had an arm around his wife's shoulder. She nestled into him, each of her arms draped over the shoulders of their children. A little boy, dressed like a soldier. He stood in present arms, a rifle strapped to his back, his hand hovering below his oversized helmet in a perpetual salute. The little girl looked hopeful, hugging a rag doll to her chest. Their white skin (for what other color could it be?), their light hair, stood out in the darkness of the lobby after hours. Lit from below, they looked like ghouls to Greer. Ghosts of war. Pale corpses held up and trotted about.

While Greer hated them, was tired of this fictional family rearing their ugly heads, he envied them. Their existence was uncomplicated, he imagined. They loved each other, and their country. He gave them all the middle finger before stepping away. Greer took the stairs down to the basement, where the Sex and Gender Divison was housed.

Made in the USA
Middletown, DE
03 September 2024

60263009R00047